So, they say you've broken the law:

Challenging Legal Authority

Author: the lioness

Published by: the lioness

Year of publication: 2011

ISBN 978-1-4709-3221-3

"To be governed is to be watched, inspected, spied upon, directed, law-driven, numbered, regulated, enrolled, indoctrinated, preached at, controlled, checked, estimated, valued, censured, commanded, by creatures who have neither the right nor the wisdom nor the virtue to do so. To be governed is to be at every operation, at every transaction noted, registered, counted, taxed, stamped, measured, numbered, assessed, licensed, authorized, admonished, prevented, forbidden, reformed, corrected, punished. It is, under pretext of public utility, and in the name of the general interest, to be placed under contribution, drilled, fleeced, exploited, monopolized, extorted from, squeezed, hoaxed, robbed; then, at the slightest resistance, the first word of complaint, to be repressed, fined, vilified, harassed, hunted down, abused, clubbed, disarmed, bound, choked, imprisoned, judged, condemned, shot, deported, sacrificed, sold, betrayed; and to crown all, mocked, ridiculed, derided, outraged, dishonored. That is government; that is it's justice; that is it's morality".

Pierre-Joseph Proudhon

Table of Contents

INTRODUCTION **5**

I AM FREEBORN, JUST LIKE YOU **7**

PROOF OF CLAIM **11**

PROOF OF AUTHORITY **15**

HOW CONSENT IS GAINED **17**

WHO HAS GENUINE AUTHORITY? **23**

THE SOCIAL CONTRACT **27**

THE VITAL DIFFERENCE **29**

EXAMPLES TO USE: **33**

LETTER TO CLAIMANT *33*

REASON FOR APPEAL *35*

DO YOU PLEAD GUILTY OR NOT GUILTY? *36*

DO YOU SWEAR TO TELL THE TRUTH, THE WHOLE TRUTH AND NOTHING BUT THE TRUTH? *37*

DEFINITIONS **39**

INTRODUCTION

This little book will give you the information required to challenge the authority of any person or entity that claims you have broken the law.

From a parking ticket to the most 'serious' legislative claim, there must be PROOF of claim.

Driving laws, Tax laws, Prohibition and Registration, all are CLAIMS made upon us. Are they founded in law, or in force? This book will help you successfully challenge the preconceived notion of AUTHORITY.

This survival guide will give you the knowhow and the tools to successfully challenge alleged AUTHORITY in and out of court.

What is LAW and what is a CLAIM?

Understand this simple concept and you (or your lawyer/barrister) will be able to defend your case appropriately.

The author has included some 'examples' that, whilst not designed to be used as templates, will give you a firm foundation for your challenge, whether on paper or verbally.

Keep this pocket-sized book with you at all times. Use it to show to anyone who makes a CLAIM upon you.

This book will tell you (and him or her) why this is important revolutionary information.

With a chapter of DEFINITIONS at the back, this book illustrates an incontrovertible POINT OF LAW that has never been used in public.

Until now …

I AM FREEBORN, JUST LIKE YOU

You wish to make a claim upon me? I have allegedly broken the law?

Do you have PROOF of CLAIM?

Do you have PROOF of AUTHORITY?

If you take any action against me from this moment on, you must be CERTAIN you can answer "yes" to the above two questions. You will be required to in court.

If the answer to the above two questions is anything other than an absolute yes, you are operating outside your professional capacity and your actions are those of a man or woman acting upon your OWN liability. Your actions will be ULTRA VIRES and you may not rely on your bond, insurance or employer to cover you for professional malpractice.

If an act requires legal authority and it is done with such authority, it is known in law as Intra Vires {the standard legal translation is WITHIN POWER}. If an act requires legal authority and it is done without such authority, it is known in law as Ultra Vires {the standard legal translation is BEYOND POWER}.

DO NOT PROCEED unless you are certain you possess the FOUNDATION EVIDENCE for your claim, because I shall summons it in court.

You will be committing the CIVIL CRIME (human against human) of TORT, including but not limited to the breach of a duty of care, a wrongful trespass against me or my property, assault, battery, false imprisonment, invasion of privacy, tortuous interference, fraud, tort conversion, intentional infliction of emotional distress (IIED), invasion of privacy, abuse of process, MALICIOUS PROSECUTION and ultimately aggravated damages of malfeasance/misfeasance in public office.

"An avidity to punish is always dangerous to liberty. It leads men to stretch, to misinterpret, and to misapply even the best of laws. He that would make his own liberty secure must guard even his enemy from oppression; for if he violates his duty, he establishes a precedent that will reach to himself".

Thomas Paine

I have not had sight of proof of claim nor proof of authority. I believe no such proof exists.

Make no mistake, in this CIVIL matter I will sue YOU PERSONALLY, not the employee/uniform status you may imagine will protect you

PROOF OF CLAIM

You have made a CLAIM upon me that I must do as you say. You allege I have broken the law.

My actions indeed may contravene some legislation but do you have irrefutable EVIDENCE that your law applies to me?

Can you show me now, or in the future, any evidence whatsoever which demonstrates that this law applies to me?

Who created this law against me?

Who pays you to take action against me to enFORCE this law?

Whoever your employer may be, arguably the ultimate alleged authority in this matter is Elizabeth, the constitutional monarch. Elizabeth is effectively the CEO of the government without whom legislation cannot be passed. All legislation in the UK requires consent of the monarch.

You have probably heard her say "my government . . ." on many occasions. It is undoubtedly HER government, but is it MY government? Do you have PROOF it is? Do you have EVIDENCE that she, or someone - anyone - anywhere - has a higher claim upon me than me?

You will be required to supply this FOUNDATION EVIDENCE in court.

Who owns me?

Who has a higher claim upon me than me?

Will Elizabeth bear witness to the fact that she allegedly owns me? If not Elizabeth herself, will a representative of the Crown Prosecution Service (CPS), the police or government bear witness that I am 'owned'?

If they were to do so, we would have a lot more to discuss, regarding SLAVERY.

An example: You have given your employer a right to make a professional CLAIM upon you in many ways: You have allowed them to give you orders; access your bank account; regulate your professional behavior. Those rules/laws apply to you because you have consented. You have entered into contract.

I HAVE NOT had sight of any proof of claim upon me. I believe no such proof exists.

PROOF OF AUTHORITY

Elizabeth demonstrates, through your actions, that she will pay you to enFORCE her rules and codes against me.

Who authorized her to do that?

Not I . . .

Elizabeth was born as free, as naked and as simply human as you and me. At some point that freeborn woman decided she would use FORCE against me if I did not comply with her rules and codes.

Monarch, King, Queen, Prince, Princess, Government, President and Prime Minister are all legal fiction titles. The real people behind those titles have no more intrinsic authority over me than the postman or a cat.

Regardless of these laws being written in the form of legislation or acts of parliament, the only thing that gives those documents authority is the consent of those who would be governed.

Simply because your employer says you may act with authority over me, does not in itself provide EVIDENCE that they, or you, have such authority. What they, or you have is FORCE, not authority.

I did not, do not and will not authorize your use of FORCE against me.

I HAVE NOT had sight of any proof authority. I believe no such proof exists.

HOW CONSENT IS GAINED

There are many ways consent can be given.

Agreement:

Simply agreeing is enough. If I allow someone power over me, I consent to his or her actions.

Voting:

The UK is allegedly a democracy. By voting for any candidate to govern me, I consent to be governed. It is as easy as that. It is equally true for my town council, county council, or something as seemingly innocuous as the local parish council. If I give my power to someone else, I consent to the resulting behavior.

The fraud, war crimes, abuse and coercion perpetrated by those in parliament means that my conscience would not allow me to sanction or be seen to condone such unlawfulness.

I will not vote for a system of government that oppresses others and me. I have no requirement for a governor.

I HAVE NOT voted for anyone.

I have attained the age of Majority, can manage my own affairs and provided that I cause no loss or harm to any other man or woman, I have committed no CRIME.

Legislation claims I have committed a crime, but I have committed an offence: Who is offended by me driving at 42 miles an hour in a 30 zone, for example? Would it offend you? Would it offend you if you were at home in bed, or watching TV or anywhere else at all? Why does it offend Elizabeth? Is she in the car with me?

I may have an accident or cause some damage to someone else or his or her car. True, I may. But I may not. To penalize someone for what *may* happen is a tort conversion.

A tort is a wrong. Conversion is the intentional exercise of dominion and control of another's property without their consent or privilege.

My body is my property.

Affirmation or Acknowledgement:

This comes in many guises. Every time someone sings those infamous words "long to reign over us . . ." they are giving away their power to Elizabeth and subsequently to her agents.

I DO NOT agree that Elizabeth has any claim to reign over me.

Obeying:

By doing what I am told without protest or under duress, I am consenting to someone being higher in status than me - no matter who that person or legal fiction entity is; and no matter what the order.

Contract:

Have I ever signed a contract, made agreement, shaken hands or made a promise? These actions are EVIDENCE that I have consented.

The law allows for all manner of corruptions on an alleged contract.

I can and will be held liable for an implied contract, or a secret contract, or trust, or agreement, or any manner of fraudulent permutations. I am construed as being in agreement if I do not express my wishes to the contrary - even when I didn't know about it.

When I do express my wishes to the contrary, I will invariably be ignored or assaulted.

There is a perfectly good reason why Elizabeth and her agents do this and get away with it. It is quite simply called FORCE:

- Elizabeth controls the government; and
- Elizabeth controls the police FORCE; and
- Elizabeth controls the other ARMED FORCEs; and
- Elizabeth controls the Ministry of Justice; and
- Elizabeth controls the Courts; and
- Elizabeth controls the Judges; and
- Elizabeth controls the Lawyers and Barristers (QUEEN's council); and
- Elizabeth signs off on all legislation; and
- Elizabeth signs off on all wars; and
- Elizabeth is permanently surrounded by a paid army sworn to protect her, her heirs and successors; and
- Elizabeth ultimately PAYS you to use FORCE against me, and it is called law.
- People pay in the form of taxes, to consent to all of the above.

I HAVE NOT had sight of any contract that evidences I have consented to be governed or policed. I believe no such proof exists.

WHO HAS GENUINE AUTHORITY?

The monarch? The government? Legislation? You? Your employer? An MP?

Many CLAIM authority over me, but where is the PROOF of that authority? Could you produce PROOF to a court? You will be required to.

Can you supply the FOUNDATION EVIDENCE for a court case, that someone, somewhere has a higher claim upon me than me? You will be required to.

Will you be able to supply a copy of an alleged contract, wherein I have granted anyone authority over me? You will be required to.

Will you be able to present a witness who has a higher claim upon me than me? You will be required to.

Will you be able to present witness evidence in any form to demonstrate that someone has a legitimately higher claim upon me than me? Again, you will be required to.

Without the consent of this human, no-other human can possibly have authority over me.

Just because you act AS IF you have authority over me does not EVIDENCE that you have such authority. What you are relying on is FORCE, not authority.

The only one able to lawfully grant you authority over me is … me.

I DO NOT CONSENT to be governed, ruled, forced or policed.

I HAVE NOT had sight of any proof of authority over me. I believe no such proof exists.

However . . . If I commit a crime of LOSS or HARM against any other man or woman (or child), they DO have lawful claim and authority to prosecute me. There is PROOF of CLAIM (I have harmed them in some way). There is PROOF OF AUTHORITY (they have a RIGHT to JUSTICE) and I should put right what I have done wrong.

I shall always be held to account for a CORPUS DELICTI (body of crime) CRIME; meaning a crime must have been proven to have occurred before I can be convicted of committing that crime.

But . . . I shall always be innocent (not 'not guilty') for any alleged offences/crimes that do not have PROOF of CLAIM or AUTHORITY (or loss).

THE SOCIAL CONTRACT

You allege I am bound by a Social Contract?

Please show me that contract. I should like to see my signature.

Perhaps you will present it in court . . . ?

An alleged social contract cannot be used as evidence of LAW to justify legislated governmental rules, because government will initiate FORCE against anyone who does not wish to enter into such a contract.

"Distrust everyone in whom the impulse to punish is powerful".

Friedrich Neitzsche

By now, I hope you are getting the picture?

I DO NOT CONSENT to be governed.

I DO NOT CONSENT to be policed.

You have NO AUTHORITY over me.

DO NOT PROCEED AGAINST ME unless you are certain you have the FOUNDATION EVIDENCE of your claim, because I shall summons it in court.

I HAVE NOT had sight of any Social Contract. I believe no such contract exists.

THE VITAL DIFFERENCE

In all court cases, other than those prosecuted by the Crown Prosecution Service (magistrates and crown court cases), there is always a requirement for the complainant to present the FOUNDATION EVIDENCE of the claim.

Example 1:

A man stops me in the street and demands that I pay him the £100 I owe him. I agree to pay, on the condition that he PROVES his claim by providing EVIDENCE that I owe him any, let alone the total amount of money claimed. He may have an IOU, but does it refer to me? Maybe it refers to someone with a similar name to me, or maybe he is just chancing his luck? Maybe he forged the document? Maybe he has a witness who saw him lend me £100? In CIVIL court, if there is no PROOF of claim, there is no claim.

Example 2:

I receive a letter from the police saying my vehicle has been speeding. I agree to pay the fine on the condition that they provide PROOF of claim ie the photographic evidence, or personal evidence of a reliable and appropriate witness - usually a police officer who saw me. Does the evidence PROVE the original speed limit on that stretch of road was less than my speed? Can they prove I was the driver? Was it my car and not a clone, etc?

What happens is the EVIDENCE relating to the CLAIM is what is argued in court; prosecution says I DID do something and defense says I DID NOT. They argue the facts of the CLAIM but they do not, ever, dispute the complete lack of EVIDENCE that they have AUTHORITY to claim against me in the first place.

"There's no way to rule innocent men. The only power government has is the power to crack down on criminals. Well, when there aren't enough criminals, one makes them. One declares so many things to be a crime that it becomes impossible for men to live without breaking laws".

Ayn Rand

- I have broken the law.
- someone has evidence that I broke the law.
- there is a witness who saw me break the law.
- law applies to me because legislation says so.
- the government says law applies to me.
- a judge says law applies to me.
- everyone has to obey the law.
- you say I am crazy . . .
- the police have written it in PACE.
- the queen says law applies to me.
- I am a member of SOCIETY.

- society says law applies to me.
- the social contract binds me to obey the law.
- if I don't like it, I can do something about it.

All the statements above are CLAIMS. They are not PROOF of a right to make a claim upon me.

The FOUNDATION EVIDENCE of all these claims is missing: There is NO PROOF of AUTHORITY.

There never can be . . .

EXAMPLES TO USE:

Letter to Claimant

[Your name and address]

[Claimant's name and address]

[Date:]

Dear [insert claimant/court name here],

Further to your [letter/notice/summons etc] dated [date] ref [their reference] I bring to your attention that the following FOUNDATION EVIDENCE for your claim is missing:

PROOF of CLAIM.

PROOF OF AUTHORITY.

If you decline to furnish me with the above information within the statutory [x] days, please be aware that I shall OBJECT in court to the complete lack of real evidence, illustrative evidence, demonstrative evidence, witness evidence or documentary evidence and will summons it accordingly.

I have not given my consent to be governed or policed.

This appears to be a tort conversion.

Please note: Legislation, Acts of Parliament, FORCE used and common practice are all claims made upon me, however they are neither PROOF of CLAIM nor PROOF of AUTHORITY. The only proof they provide is proof of FORCE.

If you choose to progress this matter, you should be aware that I shall summons witness evidence in court, demanding Proof of Claim and Proof of Authority that you (or someone, somewhere - anyone, anywhere) have a higher claim upon me than me – without my consent. I shall also file a Statutory Declaration to that effect.

Yours sincerely,

Reason for appeal

It has come to my attention that the following FOUNDATION EVIDENCE was missing:

PROOF of CLAIM.

PROOF OF AUTHORITY.

The prosecution presented no real evidence, illustrative evidence, demonstrative evidence, witness evidence or documentary evidence to the court.

I have not given my consent to be governed or policed. I also wish to file a Statutory Declaration to that effect.

The [judgment/sentence] appears to be the result of a tort conversion.

"Do you plead Guilty or Not Guilty?"

"I'm afraid I don't know, your honour(s) …

"I have not seen any FOUNDATION EVIDENCE for this claim, despite requesting it, so with the availability of neither PROOF OF CLAIM nor PROOF OF AUTHORITY I cannot *honestly* know whether I am guilty or not guilty of committing a crime when I have seen no EVIDENCE that [insert relevant legislative claim here] applies to me.

"I have not been presented with ANY preliminary material evidence in the form of exhibits or testimony of witnesses.

"This appears to be a tort conversion.

"I wish to file a Statutory Declaration to that effect, because for the court to progress this matter having been made aware that the FOUNDATION EVIDENCE is missing, would be an abuse of process".

"Do you swear to tell the truth, the whole truth and nothing but the truth?"

"Your honour(s), I am an Oathkeeper. I have sworn an oath that says I can never be compelled to swear another. It satisfies the requirements for telling the truth in court, so may I swear my oath instead?

"I, [state your name], upon my honour, do solemnly, freely and sincerely swear that in all my deeds and actions I will bear true allegiance to and protect and defend the people of this land against all enemies domestic and foreign, with fairness, integrity, diligence, honesty and impartiality, and according equal respect to all people; and that even under threat I will uphold inalienable natural rights and endeavor to prevent all crimes of loss, harm or breach of the peace against all people; and that I will to the best of my ability eliminate all forms of coercion, force, fraud and domination and discharge all these obligations thereof faithfully; and that as long as I shall live I will never under any circumstance, swear another oath".

DEFINITIONS

from OED and Wikipedia

ACT

A written law passed by Parliament, Congress, etc.

AUTHORITY

The power or right to give orders, make decisions, and enFORCE obedience.

The right to act in a specified way, delegated from one person or organization to another.

Official permission; sanction.

A person or organization having political or administrative power and control.

CERTAIN

Able to be firmly relied on to happen or be the case.

Having or showing complete conviction about something.

Without any doubt.

CLAIM

State or assert that something is the case, typically without providing evidence or proof.

An assertion that something is true.

A demand or request for something considered ones due.

A right or title to something.

COERCION

The practice of forcing another party to behave in an involuntary manner (whether through action or inaction) by use of threats, rewards, intimidation or some other form of pressure or force.

In law, coercion is codified as the duress crime.

Such actions are used as leverage, to force the victim to act in the desired way.

Coercion may involve the actual infliction of physical pain/injury or psychological harm in order to enhance the credibility of a threat.

The threat of further harm may lead to the cooperation or obedience of the person being coerced.

CONSENT

The provision of approval or assent, particularly and especially after thoughtful consideration.

a) Implied consent is a controversial form of consent, which is not expressly granted by a person, but rather inferred from a person's actions and the facts and circumstances of a particular situation (or in some cases, by a person's silence or inaction).

b) Expressed consent may be in verbal, nonverbal or written form and is clearly and unmistakably stated.

c) Verbal consent is given by using verbal communication.

d) Nonverbal consent is given by using nonverbal communication.

e) Unanimous consent, or general consent, is a parliamentary procedure.

f) Overt consent, to be valid, would require voluntariness, a specific act on the part of the consenters, a particular act consented to, and specific agents who perform this action.

g) Hypothetical consent of the governed holds that one's obligation to obey government depends on whether the government is such that one ought to consent to it, or whether the people, if placed in a state of nature without government, would agree to said government.

h) Tacit consent is the theory of an implicit social contract whereby remaining in the territory controlled by some society, which usually has a government, people give consent to join that society and be governed by its government, if any. This consent is what gives legitimacy to such government.

CONTRACT

A legally enforceable agreement between two or more parties with mutual obligations, which may or may not have elements in writing. Contracts can also be formed orally.

a) a party must have capacity to contract; and

b) the purpose of the contract must be lawful; and

c) the form of the contract must be legal; and

d) the parties must intend to create a legal relationship; and

e) the parties must consent; and

f) if a contract is in a written form, and somebody signs it, then the signatory is typically bound by its terms regardless of whether he or she has read it, provided the document is contractual in nature.

A contract must contain the following four elements:

1. **Mutual assent** - Typically this is reached through offer and acceptance, that is, when an offer is met with an acceptance that is unqualified and that does not vary the offer's terms. The latter requirement is known as the mirror image rule. If a purported acceptance does vary the terms of an offer, it is not an acceptance but a counteroffer and, therefore, simultaneously a rejection of the original offer.

2. **Offer and Acceptance** - The most important feature of a contract is that one

party makes an offer for an arrangement that another accepts. This can be called a concurrence of wills or consensus ad idem (meeting of the minds) of two or more parties. The concept is somewhat contested. The obvious objection is that a court cannot read minds and the existence or otherwise of agreement is judged objectively, with only limited room for questioning subjective intention.

3. **Consideration** - Something of value given by a promissor to a promisee in exchange for something of value given by a promisee to a promissory.

4. **Sufficiency** - Consideration must be sufficient, but courts will not weight the adequacy of consideration. For instance, agreeing to sell a car for a penny may constitute a binding contract. All that must be shown is that the seller wanted the penny. This is known as the peppercorn rule. Otherwise, the penny would constitute nominal consideration, which is insufficient.

Oral contracts are ordinarily valid and therefore legally binding. However, in most jurisdictions, certain types of contracts must be reduced to writing to be enforceable. This is to prevent frauds and perjuries.

An **implied**, unwritten, unspoken contract, also known as "a contract implied by the acts of the parties," which can be either implied in fact or implied in law, may also be legally binding.

A **bilateral** contract is an agreement in which each of the parties to the contract makes a promise or set of promises to the other party or parties - there are duties on both sides, rights on both sides, and consideration on both sides. Each side has promised to do something, and each side will get something in return for what they have done.

In a **unilateral** contract, only one party to the contract makes a promise. The requirement that acceptance be communicated to the offeror is waived unless otherwise stated in the offer. The offeree accepts by performing the condition, and the offeree's performance is also treated as the price, or consideration, for the offeror's promise. The offeror is master of the offer; it is he or she who decides whether the contract will be unilateral or bilateral. In unilateral contracts, the offer is made to the public at large.

CONVERSION

The crime of exerting unauthorized use or control of someone else's property.

The intentional exercise of dominion and control of another's property without their consent or privilege.

DURESS

A situation whereby a person performs an act as a result of violence, threat or other pressure against the person.

Any unlawful threat or coercion used ... to induce another to act [or not act] in a manner [they] otherwise would not [or would].

Pressure exerted upon a person to coerce that person to perform an act that he or she ordinarily would not perform.

EVIDENCE

The available body of facts or information indicating whether a belief or proposition is true or valid.

Information drawn from personal testimony, a document, or a material object, used to establish facts in a legal investigation or admissible as testimony in a law court.

Give information and answer questions formally and in person in a law court or at an inquiry.

FICTION

Something that is invented or untrue.

A belief or statement that is false, but is often held to be true because it is expedient to do so.

FORCE

Strength or energy as an attribute of physical action or movement.

FOUNDATION EVIDENCE

Sufficient preliminary evidence of the authenticity and relevance for the admission of material evidence in the form of exhibits or testimony of witnesses.

Material evidence is important evidence that may serve to determine the outcome of a case.

Exhibits include real evidence, illustrative evidence, demonstrative evidence, and documentary evidence.

The type of preliminary evidence necessary to lay the proper foundation depends on the form and type of material evidence offered.

The lack of foundation is a valid objection that an adverse party may raise during trial.

FREEBORN

Not born in slavery.

GOVERNMENT

The group of people with the authority to govern a country or state; a particular ministry in office.

The system by which a state or community is governed.

The action or manner of controlling or regulating a state, organization, or people.

LAW

The system of rules which a particular country or community recognizes as regulating the actions of its members and which it may enforce by the imposition of penalties.

LEGAL

Relating to the law.

Appointed or required by the law.

Recognized by common or statute law, as distinct from equity.

Permitted by law.

LEGISLATION

Laws, considered collectively.

The process of making or enacting laws.

LIABILITY

The state of being legally responsible for something.

A thing for which someone is responsible, especially an amount of money owed.

A person or thing whose presence or behavior is likely to put one at a disadvantage.

POWER

The ability or capacity to do something or act in a particular way.

Political or social authority or control, especially that exercised by a government.

Authority that is given or delegated to a person or body.

A person or organization that is strong or influential within a particular context.

PROTEST

An expression of objection, by words or by actions, to particular events, policies or situations.

PROOF

Evidence or argument establishing a fact or the truth of a statement.

Law the spoken or written evidence in a trial.

The action of establishing the truth of a statement.

SLAVE

A person who is the legal property of another and is forced to obey them.

A person who is excessively dependent upon or controlled by something.

A device, or part of one, directly controlled by another.

SOCIAL CONTRACT

An intellectual device intended to explain the appropriate relationship between individuals and their governments. Social contract arguments assert that individuals unite into political societies by a process of mutual consent, agreeing to abide by common rules and accept corresponding duties to protect themselves and one another from violence and other kinds of harm.

Printed in Great Britain
by Amazon

18558942R00031